Fall's Yield

Majestic Reflection
Devotional Study Series
Book Four

A quarterly devotional by:

J. K. Sanchez

All scripture quotations are taken from The ESV Bible (The Holy Bible, English Standard Version).

Fall's Yield: Book 4 of Majestic Reflection Devotional Study Series.
ISBN -13: 978-0692499474
ISBN – 10: 0692499474

Published by: Button Lane Books Spanaway, WA 98387
Contact: Judy@jksanchez.com - www.jksanchez.com

Cover Photography by:
Majestic Reflection-J.K.Sanchez Photography
Cover Design by:
Button Lane Books www.buttonlanebooks.com

Dedication

To those who have begun and continue to walk on this narrow path of stepping into a life journey of pursuing the presence of our Lord Jesus Christ above all other life distractions. Enjoy the journey as you enter the open door where Grace meets Lordship!

Dedication

[illegible]

Contents

Acknowledgments

First and foremost, I am thankful for the support and consistent overflow of love from my husband, Dennis, my children, their spouses and my grandchildren. My overwhelming Joy is found in each of your faces.

My continued love and appreciation to my sister, my friend, my almost TWIN in every way and my editor. Thank you Donna for always being there and knowing my thoughts before I speak them.

And finally – but above all – my thanks to Jesus Christ who directed, inspired, and taught me to enter His grace where I walk daily in His rest and assurance of His love. There I delight as I live in a new place of complete Lordship. His presence and promise of favor and abundance are always there for me.

My life is not my own but a gift freely given back to the one who gave His life for me.

<u>Introduction</u>

My passionate journey for the presence of the Lord began within me decades ago and has drawn me to a narrow path filled with promise and freedom that I have never experienced before. During this journey I have found a deep <u>knowing</u> of my true identity as a daughter of the King and His amazing love for ME. As my path has narrowed to a place of the <u>one thing</u> – His face and presence - I have learned a new depth of love, rest, contentment and delight as I now enter a journey where daily I live under His Lordship. These have shown me the importance of simplification that has brought me true freedom in Christ.

His gift on the cross is just that – a gift. All of the "I can do's" are learning to lie down as my life is becoming focused on Him and what has already been "done" for me.

This book series has been ignited directly from that love and I desire to share, direct and encourage you to a place to meet Him, love Him, hear Him, see Him and be a lover of His presence as I am.

Most devotionals are 365 days of amazing deep thoughts that honestly, most of us don't make through. We miss a few days and give it up.

This devotional study series is:

Based on a **quarter** and a 6-day week; (leaving day 7 for you to experience the filling of His presence as you gather with others).

It is **perpetual** so it can be used year after year as you walk out this journey.

It is **interactive** – it gives you a comparatively thought filled piece of writing and then builds with scripture and questions that will stir you to look deep within yourself - making this a personal growth experience.

My desire is to direct you to His feet and see His transformation materialize in your life.

ENJOY THIS AMAZING JOURNEY AS YOU ENTER INTO A DAILY WALK WHERE GRACE MEETS LORDSHIP!

“There’s No Place Like Home”

Dorothy landed in Oz with a loud thump of awakening. As she opened the door the overwhelming awareness of not being “in Kansas anymore” rang in her ears as she announced this fact to Toto.

Not being in her familiar surroundings was obvious as we watched the sepia screen erupt with brilliant full color. We too, anticipated her new journey into the unknown.

Her journey toward home began as wisdom was offered – “follow the yellow brick road”.

Her travels toward home on this long arduous road quickly began to open her eyes to who she was. Her desire for home quickly showed her how much she had been given and a longing grew that drove her to find this place called home.

Reaching the end of the yellow brick road wasn’t the end; for here she didn’t find what she expected. More was required to reach her ultimate destination. As she experienced trials and struggles she again comes to the end with nothing in hand.

Disappointment again surges and brings her to tears as finally the true answer is spoken. She finds that her way home was only a “click” away. A very simple statement of faith rang out “There’s no place like home” and she was received home with open arms.

Knowing who you are in Christ and that you are always only a "click" away from open arms of love and forgiveness makes your life journey toward home a simple statement of faith.

As you lay down your need to do it all on your own you begin to understand what yielding is all about. A statement of faith and a soft "click, click, click" is where His grace steps in and you are instantly home at His throne.

Your choices are to yield to His outstretched love ("click, click, click") and accept His forgiveness ("There's no place like home").

Day 1

Spend some time contemplating what *"There's No Place Like Home"* means to you.

1. What does this mean to you?

2. How does it apply to your life?

Journaling – writing down your thoughts, frustrations, God conversations, questions, desires, dreams and beyond is an important discipline to all areas of growth in our lives. This devotional will encourage that thought process. So write, write and write. Get a separate journal notebook and be prolific in your thoughts. Amazing things jump from the Holy Spirit out on to the page as we express ourselves.

Day 2

I John 1:9 - If we confess our sins, he is faithful and just to forgive us our sins and to cleanse us from all unrighteousness.

John 3:16 - "For God so loved the world, that he gave his only Son, that whoever believes in him should not perish but have eternal life."

Romans 10:9 – because, if you confess with your mouth that Jesus is Lord and believe in your heart that God raised him from the dead, you will be saved.

1. Have you said "good bye" to your past and laid it at the feet of Jesus? Take time with Jesus today to be free and find forgiveness.

Whether you have just decided that it was time to lay your past down and accept His free gift* or you have known Christ for many years; contemplate that gift and the victory it has brought to your life.

2. What does His gift of salvation mean in your life today?

3. How do you see His continual love and forgiveness working in your life?

*(Accepting Jesus is simply acknowledging your sin and need for forgiveness. Asking Him to forgive you and believing He died for you, that he forgives you, loves you and has the very best in store for you. It's that simple. Welcome to the Kingdom of God!)

Day 3

Ephesians 1:3-14 - Blessed be the God and Father of our Lord Jesus Christ, who has blessed us in Christ with every spiritual blessing in the heavenly places, even as he chose us in him before the foundation of the world, that we should be holy and blameless before him. In love he predestined us for adoption as sons through Jesus Christ, according to the purpose of his will, to the praise of his glorious grace, with which he has blessed us in the Beloved. In him we have redemption through his blood, the forgiveness of our trespasses, according to the riches of his grace, which he lavished upon us, in all wisdom and insight making known to us the mystery of his will, according to his purpose, which he set forth in Christ as a plan for the fullness of time, to unite all things in him, things in heaven and things on earth. In him we have obtained an inheritance, having been predestined according to the purpose of him who works all things according to the counsel of his will, so that we who were the first to hope in Christ might be to the praise of his glory. In him you also, when you heard the word of truth, the gospel of your salvation, and believed in him, were sealed with the promised Holy Spirit, who is the guarantee of our inheritance until we acquire possession of it, to the praise of his glory.

Colossians 2:13-14 - And you, who were dead in your trespasses and the uncircumcision of your flesh, God made alive together with him, having forgiven us all our trespasses, by canceling the record of debt that stood against us with its legal demands. This he set aside, nailing it to the cross.

Galatians 4:6-7 - And because you are sons, God has sent the Spirit of his Son into our hearts, crying, "Abba! Father!" So you are no longer a slave, but a son, and if a son, then an heir through God.

Knowing who you are in Christ and what He has already taken to the cross for you allows you the ability to trust in a love that was freely given on your behalf. Your heart can begin to find that voice within you that calls out Abba, Father to your heavenly Father.

1. Consider these scriptures – how do they give you a glimpse of who you are in Christ?

2. Express your own thoughts of being a child – an heir of God?

Day 4

John 14:1 - Let not your hearts be troubled. Believe in God; believe also in me.

Proverbs 13:12 – Hope deferred makes the heart sick, but <u>a desire fulfilled is a tree of life</u>.

Psalm 62:5-8 - For God alone, O my soul, wait in silence, for my hope is from him. He only is my rock and my salvation, my fortress; I shall not be shaken. On God rests my salvation and my glory; my mighty rock, my refuge is God. Trust in him at all times, O people; pour out your heart before him; God is a refuge for us. Selah

Disappointments surround us daily as we expect life to "work out". However, often it seems to bring hurdles to jump and long roads to traverse. Our desire for home (the presence of God) continues to stir up faith and growth as we persistently move forward.

1. What disappointments have you encountered this week?

2. How can you move forward through them by placing your eyes on Christ?

3. Spend time today at the feet of Jesus – leaving those disappointments and struggles.

Day 5

Jeremiah 33:3 - Call to me and I will answer you, and will tell you great and hidden things that you have not known.

Psalm 63:1 – O God, you are my God earnestly I seek you; my soul thirst for you; my flesh faints for you, as in a dry and weary land where there is no water.

Romans 8:37 – No, in all these things we are more than conquerors through him who loved us.

Matt. 6:25-34 - Therefore I tell you, do not be anxious about your life, what you will eat or what you will drink, nor about your body, what you will put on. Is not life more than food, and the body more than clothing? Look at the birds of the air: they neither sow nor reap nor gather into barns, and yet your heavenly Father feeds them. Are you not of more value than they? And which of you by being anxious can add a single hour to his span of life? And why are you anxious about clothing? Consider the lilies of the field, how they grow: they neither toil nor spin, yet I tell you, even Solomon in all his glory was not arrayed like one of these. But if God so clothes the grass of the field, which today is alive and tomorrow is thrown into the oven, will he not much more clothe you, O you of little faith?

Therefore do not be anxious, saying, 'What shall we eat?' or 'What shall we drink?' or 'What shall we wear?' For the Gentiles seek after all these things, and your heavenly Father knows that you need them all. But seek first the kingdom of God and his righteousness, and all these things will be added to you. "Therefore do not be anxious about tomorrow, for tomorrow will be anxious for itself. Sufficient for the day is its own trouble.

Your desire and longing for His presence brings about the realization of "there's no place like home". This will begin the process of a willing heart that yields and calls out for God's presence. You must come to a place that desires MORE of Him and LESS of YOU for that yielding to begin.

Letting go of your ability to take care of disappointments, to fix everything and make it all right is the beginning of "follow the yellow brick road" yielding – that brings you home.

1. What does it mean to you to yield to God?

2. Looking at your own life – how does the desire for MORE of Him and Less of You express a yielding process?

3. What areas do you find yourself always jumping into the mix to fix instead of stepping back and allowing Him?

4. Take time to lay those above areas down as you sit at His feet today.

Day 6

Re-read *"There's No Place Like Home".*

1. What have you learned this week about yielding?

2. What is one key to walking in a yielded life?

3. Write out a personal "Simple statement of faith".

You are Redeemed!

Decisions on the Yellow Brick Road

Dorothy's yellow brick road had its challenges. Crossroads and voices in this strange land seemed to pop up everywhere.

Periodically her encounter with a crossroad brought her to a place of decision. All roads looked the same but only one would bring her to Oz.

Throughout her journey, Dorothy encountered many voices – a scarecrow, a tin man, a lion, a good witch, munchkins, Oz, the wicked witch and her little Toto. Each one stirred and directed her differently. There were ones of wisdom, love, peace, joy, silent loyalty, fear, anger, manipulation and intimidation. Listening to each of these voices brought either a positive or negative interaction into the story and directed the stories flow on that yellow brick road.

You too, find your life journey peppered with crossroads as well as many voices calling out directions.

Each crossroad you encounter declares a defining moment in your life. The choices made at these times determine your ultimate pre-planned purpose and can affect the rest of your life. If you allow Jesus to BE Lord in those moments you will make it to the end of your journey – your Oz – seeing His amazing faithfulness in all areas.

The voices that inundate your journey and direct your crossroads will ultimately help or hurt you spiritually - not only during those crossroad decision times but also on a daily basis. Learning to listen to only those voices that will strengthen God's plan in your life is a process of choice.

Of those many voices God has placed in your life, many will encourage and direct you with wisdom. However, the ultimate voice to direct your decisions must be the voice of your Lord. Learning that voice means spending time at His feet.

Crossroads will come; voices will speak – BUT only Christ - the one road - will bring you to the place and purpose He has for your life.

Day 1

Spend some time contemplating what ***Decisions on the Yellow Brick Road*** means to you.

1. What does this mean to you?

2. How does it apply to your life?

Day 2

Proverbs 18:24 – A man of many companions may come to ruin, but there is a friend who sticks closer than a brother.

Proverbs 11:14 - Where there is no guidance, a people falls, but in an abundance of counselors there is safety.

1 Corinthians 15:33 - Do not be deceived: "Bad company ruins good morals."

Proverbs 15:22 – Without counsel plans fail, but with many advisers they succeed.

The voices of those that surround you can bring a positive life giving influence and direction to your life. However, there are also those voices of well meaning individuals that will often pour out opinions that if followed can bring destruction to your life. Finding those who "speak life" and give direction with wisdom is imperative.

1. Do you have voices in your life that speak life and wisdom or ones that speak confusion and chaos?

2. Make a list of positive and negative voices in your life.

3. Spending time with positive life giving people always will bring you life. How can you adjust the negative voices of influence in your life?

Day 3

Proverbs 12:15 - The way of a fool is right in his own eyes, but a wise man listens to advice.

Proverbs 19:20 - Listen to advice and accept instruction, that you may gain wisdom in the future.

Romans 12:2 - Do not be conformed to this world, but be transformed by the renewal of your mind, that by testing you may discern what is the will of God, what is good and acceptable and perfect.

1 Corinthians 10:13 - No temptation has overtaken you that is not common to man. God is faithful, and he will not let you be tempted beyond your ability, but with the temptation he will also provide the way of escape, that you may be able to endure it.

Crossroads in your life bring you to a place of often agonizing decisions. "Do I move, do I take this job, do I love this person, do I ….." They are times where your choices are defining moments for your life. Right or wrong – they will change your life.

No one can make these decisions for you. Those you surround yourself with are the advisors that will ultimately help you decide the answer. Your choice of whom you listen to is of utmost importance.

1. What defining moment decisions are you facing now?

2. Who are you counting on for input in this decision?

3. Take time today to sit at the feet of Jesus. Take these decisions to Him. Listen for His voice in confirming or re-directing you in your choice. Journal your "God Time' thoughts.

Day 4

Psalm 19:7-10 - The law of the LORD is perfect, reviving the soul; the testimony of the LORD is sure, making wise the simple; the precepts of the LORD are right, rejoicing the heart; the commandment of the LORD is pure, enlightening the eyes; the fear of the LORD is clean, enduring forever; the rules of the LORD are true, and righteous altogether. More to be desired are they than gold, even much fine gold; sweeter also than honey and drippings of the honeycomb.

Proverbs 8:32-35 – "And now, O sons, listen to me: blessed are those who keep my ways. Hear instruction and be wise, and do not neglect it. Blessed is the one who listens to me, watching daily at my gates, waiting beside my doors. For whoever finds me finds life and obtains favor from the Lord,

2 Thessalonians 3:3 - But the Lord is faithful. He will establish you and guard you against the evil one.

I Corinthians 14:33 – For God is not a God of confusion but of peace.

Philippians 4:7 – And the peace of God, which surpasses all understanding, will guard your hearts and minds in Christ Jesus.

Ultimately all decisions made in a yielded life are made at the feet of Jesus. Hearing His voice is the one sure way of finding and following His perfect laid out plan for your life. There is no quick fix to hearing that voice – it's found only in a yielded vessel that waits in His presence. Then peace will reign as you move into those decisions. If chaos and confusion are present – wait – His decisions and direction will bring an assurance and peace. There is no promise of easy - just a promise of knowing deep inside a peace that passes all understanding.

1. As you have made decisions in the past – what has been your process to make them?

2. Have you experienced peace or chaos in those times?

3. If this is a new process for you - How can you apply it to decisions you are making currently? If you have walked this process before – How can you deepen that walk?

4. Spend time today at the feet of Jesus – listening in silence as you wait on Him. Journal your time.

Day 5

1 Thessalonians 5:24 - He who calls you is faithful; he will surely do it.

Lamentations 3:22-23 - The steadfast love of the LORD never ceases; his mercies never come to an end; they are new every morning; great is your faithfulness.

Colossians 3:2 - Set your minds on things that are above, not on things that are on earth.

Psalm 40:8 – "I delight to do your will, O my God; your law is within my heart."

The faithfulness of Christ in your life will bring you to and through all crossroads and decisions that present themselves in your life. Standing on His faithfulness will never disappoint you.

Trusting that He always is there, always loves you and has a purpose for your life will bring you to the end of your journey with an assurance of fulfilling your assignment.

1. Look at your life and list at lease 5 places you currently see the faithfulness of Christ?

2. Spend time today rejoicing in His faithfulness. Journal your time.

Day 6

Re-read *Decisions on the Yellow Brick Road.*

Proverbs 16:9 - The heart of man plans his way, but the LORD establishes his steps.

Psalm 119:10 - With my whole heart I seek you; let me not wander from your commandments!

1. How will a yielded heart allow decisions and crossroad experiences to catapult you into His purposes?

2. What insights have you found this week?

3. Journal any thoughts that the Holy Spirit stirred as you re-read this weeks prose.

You are Created for His Purposes!

Freedom Flows Under His Reign

The resounding thunderous roar of a forceful waterfall erupts over a precipice bringing a surge of awe within our beings.

However, the formation of this mighty eruption begins quite differently. It begins as a trickle.

Over time, that trickle of water strengthens as its determination grows and solidifies its purpose.

Depth and width grow from a trickle, to ankle deep, knee deep, waist deep as its purpose expands. Only then when it is deep enough to swim in does the fun begin. Force begins to operate and the very terrain around it is changed as it makes its path. Often powerfully carving out its way through solid rock.

Its out-pouring and exclamation of freedom and purpose find its expression as it releases all of nature's boundaries and erupts out into its environment bringing life and change.

The free gift of grace poured out to us through Christ is like the formation of a new waterfall. The trickle released to us is His forgiveness. As with parched ground our hearts receive it and we are refreshed. Freedom erupts.

This eruption allows the trickle to grow into a deeper and faster source of water. That growth requires accepting His lordship in our lives. This place opens our eyes and ears to what He has called us to. It shows us the path and directs the way to pass through solid rock.

As we grow from acceptance of grace into a place of Lordship we step into a new place of freedom.

Grace and Lordship release us to walk into a place where the freedom to flow out and cascade with exuberance into His purposes becomes possible. It's a place where we live in freedom under the reign of Christ.

As we live daily walking under His reign we are able to become that resounding thunderous roar of a waterfall as we release all we are created to be into our environment. This is the place we have been called to - the place where heaven touches earth.

Join me as we begin that free flow over the precipice and into the depths of our calling.

Day 1

Spend some time contemplating what *Freedom Flows Under His Reign* means to you.

1. What does this mean to you?

2. How does it apply to your life?

Day 2

Ephesians 2:4-6 - But God, being rich in mercy, because of the great love with which he loved us, even when we were dead in our trespasses, made us alive together with Christ—by grace you have been saved—and raised us up with him and seated us with him in the heavenly places in Christ Jesus,

Ephesians 2:13 - But now in Christ Jesus you who once were far off have been brought near by the blood of Christ.

The amazing gift of grace that Christ paid for on the cross is the beginning of a freedom that changes you and opens the door to heaven. However, that is the beginning; you have been given an immense inheritance that allows a life walked in newfound purpose.

1. What does the "gift of grace" mean to you?

2. Spend time today journaling your understanding of God's love for you.

Day 3

Galatians 2:20 - I have been crucified with Christ. It is no longer I who live, but Christ who lives in me And the life I now live in the flesh I live by faith in the Son of God, who loved me and gave himself for me.

Jeremiah 24:7 - I will give them a heart to know that I am the LORD, and they shall be my people and I will be their God, for they shall return to me with their whole heart.

1 John 4:16 - So we have come to know and to believe the love that God has for us. God is love, and whoever abides in love abides in God, and God abides in him.

Upon the understanding of the great gift of grace given to you, you will enter into an awareness of His love for you. The awareness begins as a trickle and soon grows as you breathe in and out. That love that now saturates and infuses you brings a flood of change. The more you sit in His presence you are filled with love. The more love you receive the more you will desire to place Him in a position of Lordship in your life. That placement requires your decision to let go of everything and place Him as number one.

This cycle is a life long journey – you never have enough or reach the end of growing in His grace or His love. The placement of Christ as Lord in your life will always be a growing process as well – you are human and will daily struggle with taking control; thus placing Christ, as Lord is a daily yielding decision.

1. Where do you see yourself TODAY in this process – beginning to understand grace, accepting and growing in His love or placing Him as Lord?

2. What areas are the hardest for you to yield to His Lordship?

3. Spend time at the feet of Jesus today – yield those areas to His Lordship as you pray and sit in His presence. Journal your thoughts.

<u>Day 4</u>

John 8:31-32 - So Jesus said to the Jews who had believed him, "If you abide in my word, you are truly my disciples, and you will know the truth, and the truth will set you free."

II Corinthians 3:17 - Now the Lord is the Spirit, and where the Spirit of the Lord is, there is freedom.

Romans 15:13 – May the God of hope fill you with all joy and peace in believing, so that by the power of the Holy Spirit you may abound in hope.

Freedom comes as you yield to the Lordship of Jesus. What is released to you is a life walking in peace and joy unspeakable. That joy pours forth to those around you and is a source of life within your environment. You begin to see and move forward toward the plans and purposes of Gods design for your life.

1. Mediating means to ruminate – or to chew on. Take time today to "chew on" these scriptures. Journal any revelations that present themselves to you.

2. Spend time at the feet of Jesus – listen to His voice. Journal any "God thoughts" about freedom, yielding, Lordship, peace and joy.

Day 5

Proverbs 16:3 - Commit your work to the LORD, and your plans will be established.

Ezekiel 47:1-12 - Then he brought me back to the door of the temple, and behold, water was issuing from below the threshold of the temple toward the east (for the temple faced east). The water was flowing down from below the south end of the threshold of the temple, south of the altar. Then he brought me out by way of the north gate and led me around on the outside to the outer gate that faces toward the east; and behold, the water was trickling out on the south side. Going on eastward with a measuring line in his hand, the man measured a thousand cubits, and then led me through the water, and it was ankle-deep. Again he measured a thousand, and led me through the water, and it was knee-deep. Again he measured a thousand, and led me through the water, and it was waist-deep. Again he measured a thousand, and it was a river that I could not pass through, for the water had risen. It was deep enough to swim in, a river that could not be passed through. And he said to me, "Son of man, have you seen this?" Then he led me back to the bank of the river. As I went back, I saw on the bank of the river very many trees on the one side and on the other.

And he said to me, "This water flows toward the eastern region and goes down into the Arabah, and enters the sea; when the water flows into the sea, the water will become fresh. And wherever the river goes, every living creature that swarms will live, and there will be very many fish. For this water goes there, that the waters of the sea may become fresh; so everything will live where the river goes. Fishermen will stand beside the sea. From Engedi to Eneglaim it will be a place for the spreading of nets. Its fish will be of very many kinds, like the fish of the Great Sea. But its swamps and marshes will not become fresh; they are to be left for salt. And on the banks, on both sides of the river, there will grow all kinds of trees for food. Their leaves will not wither, nor their fruit fail, but they will bear fresh fruit every month, because the water for them flows from the sanctuary. Their fruit will be for food, and their leaves for healing."

Revelation 22:1-2 - Then the angel showed me the river of the water of life, bright as crystal, flowing from the throne of God and of the Lamb through the middle of the street of the city; also, on either side of the river, the tree of life with its twelve kinds of fruit, yielding its fruit each month. The leaves of the tree were for the healing of the nations.

As you yield to the Lordship of Christ in your life you will begin to reign in life and begin to walk under His plans and purposes. Those purposes impact your life as well as those you have influence with. His design for you is to be a tree of life that brings healing to those you encounter.

1. As you walk in this process – bringing life and healing wherever you go – who are those that you desire to impact?

2. Are you effective in their lives now?

3. How can you increase that?

4. Where else would you like to see your life impact others?

5. Spend time listening for direction as to your assignments of life and healing to others. Journal those thoughts.

Day 6

Matthew 22:37-39 - And he said to him, "You shall love the Lord your God with all your heart and with all your soul and with all your mind. This is the great and first commandment. And a second is like it: You shall love your neighbor as yourself.

Re-read *Freedom Flows Under His Reign.*

1. Summarize your thoughts about this weeks study?

2. What did the Holy Spirit reveal to you personally this week?

You Reign in Freedom through Christ!

Nature's Nudging

As summer begins its transition to fall nature begins to vibrate with a keen awareness. Trees, flowers, birds and squirrels are all attentively on alert. They have an internal ear that is tuned into changes that need to be heeded as this shift takes place. This awareness is a simple nudging presented by nature.

Leaves begin to shed and petals fall. Birds and squirrels hear the call to prepare in active obedience to natures encouraging love tap and they move into action. Seeds and nuts are diligently gathered and stored. Busyness vibrates in the air as anticipation quivers within.

They listen attentively and in obedience respond to that internal awareness. They obey and do what is needed to prepare for the season.

As we continue our spiritual walk – understanding the grace that Christ's blood provided and placing our lives under His lordship we then begin to hear His voice. Obedience no longer sounds like a demand or expectation. We begin to step under the flow of His reign and attentively listen for His call.

Just as a servant waits at the door expecting to be available to the requests of the King – so should our hearts lean toward that door with anticipation.

Obedience flows from a heart that is saturated in the love and presence of Jesus. Being "sold out" to His directions, plans and purposes allows for the development of a fine tuned ear that hears His call.

Our response is not determined by our own agendas but flows out of love with no hesitation. The call to action brings a quick "Yes Lord".

Join me in the call to action; as we pursue becoming attentive servants who listen and obey our Lords voice from a life filled with abundant love for our Lord and King - Jesus.

Day 1

Spend some time contemplating what *Nature's Nudging* means to you.

1. What does this mean to you?

2. How does it apply to your life?

Day 2

Titus 3:4-7 - But when the goodness and loving kindness of God our Savior appeared, he saved us, not because of works done by us in righteousness, but according to his own mercy, by the washing of regeneration and renewal of the Holy Spirit, whom he poured out on us richly through Jesus Christ our Savior, so that being justified by his grace we might become heirs according to the hope of eternal life.

II Corinthians 5:14-15 - For the love of Christ controls us, because we have concluded this: that one has died for all, therefore all have died; and he died for all, that those who live might no longer live for themselves but for him who for their sake died and was raised.

Galatians 5:6 - For in Christ Jesus neither circumcision nor uncircumcision counts for anything, but only faith working through love.

I Peter 5:6-7 – Humble yourselves, therefore, under the might hand of God so that at the proper time he may exalt you, casting all your anxieties on him, because he cares for you.

When you yield to the Lordship of Christ the non-hesitant expression of love becomes automatic. The more you yield under His reign of love the more His abundant care pours out on you. It is an amazing cycle of His love and goodness.

1. What is the difference to you between "humbling yourself" and "accepting Christ's Lordship over your life'?

2. Spend time with the Lord today expressing your love for Him. Journal your thoughts about His love and goodness toward you.

Day 3

II Corinthians 1:20 - For all the promises of God find their Yes in him. That is why it is through him that we utter our Amen to God for his glory.

Matthew 6:33 - But seek first the kingdom of God and his righteousness, and all these things will be added to you.

Isaiah 6:8 – And I heard the voice of the Lord saying, "Whom shall I send, and who will go for us?" Then I said, "Here I am! Send me."

Galatians 1:10 - For am I now seeking the approval of man, or of God? Or am I trying to please man? If I were still trying to please man, I would not be a servant of Christ.

Being an attentive obedient listener requires an unflinching attitude of "hear it and do it". This attitude is the "Yes Lord" of unhesitant love that is expressed as a servant of Christ.

1. Have you experienced a time when you felt the prompting of the Holy Spirit to do something that might have been uncomfortable? Did you do it? Share your experience.

2. Are you willing to experience more times of "hearing it and doing it"?

3. Spend time in His presence today expressing your thoughts about this and journal that "God Time".

Day 4

John 15:4-5 - Abide in me, and I in you. As the branch cannot bear fruit by itself, unless it abides in the vine, neither can you, unless you abide in me. I am the vine; you are the branches. Whoever abides in me and I in him, he it is that bears much fruit, for apart from me you can do nothing.

1 Peter 1:13 - Therefore, preparing your minds for action, and being sober-minded, set your hope fully on the grace that will be brought to you at the revelation of Jesus Christ.

Romans 10:17 – So faith comes from hearing, and hearing through the word of Christ.

John 16:13 – When the Spirit of truth comes, he will guide you into all the truth, for he will not speak on his own authority, but whatever he hears he will speak, and he will declare to you the things that are to come.

Hearing the voice of God comes in several ways. The confirmation of His direction comes from your time in the Bible, your time hearing the spoken word - sermons from your personal place of worship and from the Holy Spirit who speaks to your mind and spirit. Time is required. There is no quick learning of this process. It is a life journey where walking continually in a yielded "Yes Lord" position will produce a finely tuned ear to hear His voice.

1. Consider the above scriptures and journal thoughts that are stirred up during that time.

2. Take time today at His feet to listen. Be still in His presence and journal any "God Thoughts" from that time.

Day 5

Jeremiah 7:23 - But this command I gave them: 'Obey my voice, and I will be your God, and you shall be my people. And walk in all the way that I command you, that it may be well with you.'

Luke 12:35-36 - "Stay dressed for action and keep your lamps burning, and be like men who are waiting for their master to come home from the wedding feast, so that they may open the door to him at once when he comes and knocks.

The very word obedience often stirs a negative reaction. However, one understanding of obedience is to follow a direct action because of a love for that individual. It is out of love – not fear.

As you grow from walking in grace into a yielded position under Christ's Lordship your love for Him changes your desires. Your desires become fine-tuned to His voice and His direction. With that comes an attitude of obedience and you become a lover who is "sold out" in love with your Lord. You listen and obey. You say "Yes Lord" and "Send Me".

1. How do you perceive the word obedience? Does that understanding come out of love or fear?

2. How can you stir up and grow deeper into a place of an attentive servant for Christ?

3. Have you heard a specific direction that He has spoken to you this week? If so, what steps can you take to pursue that?

Day 6

Re-read *Nature's Nudging.*

1. As you have focused this week on being an obedient attentive listener what revelations has God stirred within you?

You are a Child of the King!

Nature's Surrender
The Last Lonely Leaves

As the days of fall become shorter and cooler we witness a beautiful example of nature's surrender.

I sit looking out at a grove of enormous maple trees that have provided a canopy of coolness throughout a scorching summer.

Now change is in the air. Cooler breezes and diminishing light begin a new season for the maple. Her leaves surrender to the process as pigment changes begin to dance within each one. Brilliant greens fade into yellows and within days some of those yellows transform to oranges and then reds. Again, over time these vivid beauties give way to browns that quickly signal finality to summer's delight.

The abundance of swaying leaves above will eventually yield to the flight that will land them at our feet. Each of the thousands of leaves will disconnect and yield to this falling process. Each leaf will enter this routine movement at different times and due to different circumstances. The end is always the same. They must end up yielding to natures call to lie down.

As I watch this falling process throughout several weeks I find myself contemplating. Some of the first leaves to let go are still green with just the slightest hints of yellow. They gracefully float to the ground creating the beginning of a soft carpet that will usher in the changes to come.

Then, as time progresses those that are yellow transform into orange and red and are then are shaken lose as winds and rains push and pull them from their previous anchors. They land unceremoniously with a "plop" upon the awaiting soggy ground.

Finally, as the maples nakedness has progressed I see the only leaves left hanging amidst her branches are now brown and dried. However, they still hold on tight. These final leaves refuse to yield to the process. But, the process will prevail.

The next storm approaches and those last lonely leaves are forced to resign to it and in the end they land with a "crunch" on the cold solid ground.

Just as these fall leaves follow a pre-determined yielding process so is there a spiritual yielding process that we experience that can be looked at similarly.

As we are presented with the decision of allowing Jesus the position of "Lordship" in our lives we too must determine how we step into that process. Do we quickly yield – saying "Yes Lord"? Do we take our time "working at it" first? Or do we "hang on" and "fight to the end" before we take that step?

Most of us will find ourselves walking in and out of these processes. So, lets flip this and start this week with the last one.

Let's look at those brown single lonely dried up leaves that are "hanging on" and going to "fight to the end" before they will yield their lives to anyone.

Now, most of you would say, "Oh - that's not me" but think again.

Whether you have been in or out of church your whole life you have heard the mind set that our society touts as beneficial in order to be a strong independent individual –we don't give up, we fight to the end, we don't need any help, and on and on it goes. So if you have grown up with that thinking, then the process of totally yielding to anyone – including Jesus can be a complete paradigm shift for you.

Many of us think we have already yielded to Jesus when we accepted Him as savior but often we have held back from the completeness of that salvation by hanging onto the branches of our previous tree. Meaning that our old thoughts and ways have continued to influence our Christian life.

Often we are so caught up in our own lives that we have become dried up and brittle. Our spirituality consists of maybe hearing a sermon once a week and going through the motions the rest of the week.

We are walking a life that is far from His desire. We don't live a life where Christ is reigning in our lives in freedom because we are not allowing HIS LORDSHIP in our life.

Our ways, our desires, our wants, our needs, our offenses - these and many others are all pieces of who we are and they need to come under HIS LORDSHIP.

His grace paid for it all – we don't need to carry any of it and we can't control anything anyways so why not just say "Yes, Lord" and let all of - <u>Our Stuff</u> - go. His Grace + His Lordship = complete freedom and a yielded moldable life ready to be poured out.

Let's allow the mindset of "hang on" and "fight to the end" to be released at the feet of Jesus.

Day 1

Spend some time contemplating what *Nature's Surrender – The Last Lonely Leaves* means to you.

1. What does this mean to you?

2. How does it apply to your life?

Day 2

Romans 7:22 – For I delight in the law of God, in my inner being.

Psalm 119:18 - Open my eyes, that I may behold wondrous things out of your law.

Psalm 68:6 - God settles the solitary in a home; he leads out the prisoners to prosperity, but the rebellious dwell in a parched land.

Living a life that goes through the motions of Christianity is not the life that His blood paid for. Finding delight in His presence and His word begins the process of a returning to a place of freedom in Christ.

If you find yourself living in a parched land look again to the refreshing that only comes from His spirit.

How do you get there? Realizing that you need Him, resting in His presence at His feet, basking in an assurance of His love for you, delighting in Him and Yielding all the old ways.

1. What areas of your life feel parched and lonely?

2. What keys above might re-direct those areas to become flourishing again?

3. Apply those keys as you spend time in the presence of Jesus today. Journal your thoughts.

Day 3

II Corinthians 4:7 - But we have this treasure in jars of clay, to show that the surpassing power belongs to God and not to us.

Isaiah 64:8 - But now, O LORD, you are our Father; we are the clay, and you are our potter; we are all the work of your hand.

You have been given amazing treasures within this life but often they are taken for granted. Running your own course as it seems fit to you. This course ends up bringing stress and struggles that He never planned for your life. Acknowledging that He is the creator and you are the created brings a deep peace that shouts – "I give up".

1. Where do you find yourself "running your own course"?

2. Does that course bring peace or stress in your life?

3. What areas may be areas where you (the clay) may be trying to direct God (the potter)'s hand?

4. Take time to sit at His feet and let them all go. Journal your thoughts.

Day 4

Ezekiel 36:26 - And I will give you a new heart, and a new spirit I will put within you. And I will remove the heart of stone from your flesh and give you a heart of flesh.

Matthew 9:17 – Neither is new wine put into old wineskins. If it is, the skins burst and the wine is spilled and the skins are destroyed. But new wine is put into fresh wineskins and so both are preserved.

II Corinthians 5:17 Therefore, if anyone is in Christ, he is a new creation. The old has passed away; behold, the new has come.

You are promised through the blood of Christ NEWNESS. He is always available with transformation and a new fresh start every time you call out and yield to His Lordship.

1. Ponder the above scriptures and allow the Holy Spirit to stir your heart. As you have cast off many areas this week consider what it means to receive NEWNESS in your spirit. Journal your thoughts.

2. Rejoice in those today.

Day 5

Isaiah 58:13-14 - "If you turn back your foot from the Sabbath, from doing your pleasure on my holy day, and call the Sabbath a delight and the holy day of the LORD honorable; if you honor it, not going your own ways, or seeking your own pleasure, or talking idly; then you shall take delight in the LORD, and I will make you ride on the heights of the earth; I will feed you with the heritage of Jacob your father, for the mouth of the LORD has spoken."

Isaiah 32:17 - And the effect of righteousness will be peace, and the result of righteousness, quietness and trust forever.

Proverbs 3:5-6 - Trust in the LORD with all your heart, and do not lean on your own understanding. In all your ways acknowledge him, and he will make straight your paths.

Changing places from being a Last Lonely Leaf to one that quickly yields requires a place of release in your life. Letting Christ be Lord in every circumstance and area of your life is a process of continually stopping first - waiting, listening and saying "Yes Lord".

1. As you walk through your day today allow a conscious thought process to surface. A thought process that is aware of situations and circumstances as they are presented. Then you chose to – stop, wait, listen and say "Yes Lord". Journal this experience.

Day 6

Re-read *Nature's Surrender – The Last Lonely Leaves.*

1. What new revelations from God did you receive this week as you spent time in His presence, worked through the questions and journaled your thoughts?

2. Can you apply this directly to your daily life? If so - where?

You are a NEW Creation in Christ!

Nature's Surrender
Those "Holding On" to Full Color

The grand display of colors that present themselves to us as the beauty of fall unfolds now brings us back to contemplate the changing color process.

By the time we see the bright orange and reds of our maple tree she has already lost many leaves that yielded earlier.

These that are now present are the leaves who have gone through the summer, adjusted to the yellowing and now have embraced full on color change and are holding on and walking through it all.

As we apply a spiritual comparison remember our desire is for surrendering at the feet of Jesus.

We are looking at a brilliant leaf that has accepted its place, its position, its role and it is walking and working just as expected in order to complete what it was set up for. Right? Right.

BUT – that's the snag!

At first thought these brilliant colorful leaves would be my preference to be. However, learning to walk under the true Lordship of Christ requires something different.

We have been taught both in and out of the church to "find your place, find your role and work hard to achieve" Work, work, work and more work.

However, what we accomplish or don't accomplish doesn't matter to Jesus. He already loved you so much that He gave his life for you and there is nothing that will change that. You do NOT earn anything by working or doing anything for Him. He doesn't need anything from you.

Once you understand that place of undeserved favor – called grace; then you can accept Him and place Him in a position of Lordship over your life where with joy and freedom you will move into a new place. Here your only desire is to hear and obey when He speaks.

Let's take time to lie down all the "busyness". Let's stop "working" to prove anything. Now let's surrender to the process of making Jesus the Lord over our life.

Day 1

Spend some time contemplating what *Nature's Surrender – Those "Holding On" to Full Color* means to you.

1. What does this mean to you?

2. How does it apply to your life?

Day 2

Isaiah 43:10-11 - "You are my witnesses," declares the LORD, "and my servant whom I have chosen, that you may know and believe me and understand that I am he. Before me no god was formed, nor shall there be any after me. I, I am the LORD, and besides me there is no savior.

Ephesians 1:3-10 - Blessed be the God and Father of our Lord Jesus Christ, who has blessed us in Christ with every spiritual blessing in the heavenly places, even as he chose us in him before the foundation of the world, that we should be holy and blameless before him. In love he predestined us for adoption as sons through Jesus Christ, according to the purpose of his will, to the praise of his glorious grace, with which he has blessed us in the Beloved. In him we have redemption through his blood, the forgiveness of our trespasses, according to the riches of his grace, which he lavished upon us, in all wisdom and insight making known to us the mystery of his will, according to his purpose, which he set forth in Christ as a plan for the fullness of time, to unite all things in him, things in heaven and things on earth.

Colossians 1:19-20 - For in him all the fullness of God was pleased to dwell, and through him to reconcile to himself all things, whether on earth or in heaven, making peace by the blood of his cross.

The blood of Jesus paid our way – 100% - into the presence of God. His love and mercy provided a poured out sacrifice of undeserved favor for all of those that call on His name and receive it. Understanding the enormity of that gift brings freedom and nothing else is required of us.

1. How would you express your personal understanding of what the Grace of God means in your life?

2. Spend time today at the feet of Jesus in an attitude of gratitude. Journal your "God Time" thoughts.

Day 3

Matthew 11:28-30 - Come to me, all who labor and are heavy laden, and I will give you rest. Take my yoke upon you, and learn from me, for I am gentle and lowly in heart, and you will find rest for your souls. For my yoke is easy, and my burden is light."

Luke 12:27 - Consider the lilies, how they grow: they neither toil nor spin, yet I tell you, even Solomon in all his glory was not arrayed like one of these.

I Peter 5:7 – casting all your anxieties on him, because he cares for you.

1 Corinthians 3:7-9 - So neither he who plants nor he who waters is anything, but only God who gives the growth. He who plants and he who waters are one, and each will receive his wages according to his labor. For we are God's fellow workers. You are God's field, God's building.

Peace is the first thing that disappears when stress arrives. A lifestyle that runs, runs and runs; whether it is "for ministry" or for life in general produces the same thing – exhausted, stressed and empty people. His plan is not for you to walk a daily lifestyle of anxiety but one filled with peace and rest in His presence.

His yoke – plans and purposes for your life – is easy. As we walk in a yielded listening position under His Lordship we begin a walk under His reign. Here our lives – even when busy – produce life and fruit that is obvious.

1. Consider your every day lifestyle – is it one of busyness and stress or one of fruitful God directed endeavors and peace?

2. How can you apply a lifestyle change that will bring about rest and peace?

3. Apply one of those changes.

Day 4

Ephesians 2:8-10 - For by grace you have been saved through faith. And this is not your own doing; it is the gift of God, not a result of works, so that no one may boast. For we are his workmanship, created in Christ Jesus for good works, which God prepared beforehand, that we should walk in them.

Romans 11:6 - But if it is by grace, it is no longer on the basis of works; otherwise grace would no longer be grace.

Galatians 2:16 - yet we know that a person is not justified by works of the law but through faith in Jesus Christ, so we also have believed in Christ Jesus, in order to be justified by faith in Christ and not by works of the law, because by works of the law no one will be justified.

Zechariah 4:6 - Then he said to me, "This is the word of the LORD to Zerubbabel: Not by might, nor by power, but by my Spirit, says the LORD of hosts.

As you chose a gift for one you love they never need to prove to you that they deserve that gift. It is out of love for them that you have decided to purchase it.

However, the free gift of grace offered to you in love often is received with a mentality that begins a cycle of proving worthiness for that gift. Setting that mentality aside requires a conscious decision and a yielding to Christ's Lordship on a daily basis.

You will never be good enough by your works – because He made you eternally good enough by His blood. You will never be able to do enough good works to pay Him back– because He did it all at the cross for YOU.

1. Take time today to contemplate the above scriptures. Chose one that speaks directly to your heart and explain why?

2. Sit at the feet of Jesus today and let go of all the "trying" mentality. Journal your thoughts.

Day 5

Hosea 6:6 - "For I desire steadfast love and not sacrifice, the knowledge of God rather than burnt offerings."

Luke 10:38-42 - Now as they went on their way, Jesus entered a village. And a woman named Martha welcomed him into her house. And she had a sister called Mary, who sat at the Lord's feet and listened to his teaching. But Martha was distracted with much serving. And she went up to him and said, "Lord, do you not care that my sister has left me to serve alone? Tell her then to help me." But the Lord answered her, "Martha, Martha, you are anxious and troubled about many things, but one thing is necessary. Mary has chosen the good portion, which will not be taken away from her."

The daily distractions of life were part of both Martha and Mary's worlds but Mary made a choice to STOP and sit at the feet of Jesus – her Lord. Did all the serving get taken care of? Not like Martha felt was necessary. But Jesus thought differently.

You need to tune your spiritual ears away from the busyness of life and listen to the whisper of the Holy Spirit as He beckons you to come away and sit.

Resting, listening and worshiping at the feet of Jesus will allow the process of full surrender to the outstretched arms of Jesus to become a lifestyle.

1. The whisper of the Holy Spirit guides and directs us daily if we listen. Take time today to stop, sit and listen.

2. Journal thoughts or directions that you heard today as you waited on the Lord.

Day 6

Re-read *Nature's Surrender – Those "Holding On" to Full Color.*

1. During this week how has your faith been stirred and stretched to lean on Grace - learning to lay down all attempts to prove yourself and to surrender to the love of Christ at His feet?

You are Made Perfect by His Blood!

Nature's Surrender
Early Yielders

With the first cooling breeze of fall begins a rustle in the waiting leaves of our maple trees. An anticipation of what is to come wiggles at the tips and stems of the leaves that expectantly wait for the first call. The first breeze lifts several leaves as they willingly detach from the limbs of the maples outstretched arms. With amazing grace they flutter unhindered through the air and land with a soft release as the beginning of fall's carpet quietly materializes.

As we again apply a spiritual comparison between these leaves and our lives - let's consider our own willingness to surrender.

Waiting and anticipation require a process of listening, which requires a place of quiet.

Willingness to step into a place with expectation is part of the acceptance of surrender.

Just as these first leaves of fall take flight we must be ready and anticipate His call. That type of yielding comes from a place of trusting Him beyond all others and knowing His voice when He calls.

Join me as we willingly detach and lie down in full surrender to His call.

Day 1

Spend some time contemplating what *Nature's Surrender – Early Yielders* means to you.

1. What does this mean to you?

2. How does it apply to your life?

Day 2

Matthew 13:44 - "The kingdom of heaven is like treasure hidden in a field, which a man found and covered up. Then in his joy he goes and sells all that he has and buys that field."

Psalm 51:12 – Restore to me the joy of your salvation, and uphold me with a willing spirit.

A life saturated in the love of Jesus will spring forth with abundant joy. That joy will place you in a position that is willing to "sell it all" for all that is available.

1. Are you abounding in joy and willing to lay down all at His feet?

2. Are there areas that still whisper "this is mine and I'm in control of it"? If so how can you take steps to detach that thinking and place them under His Lordship?

Day 3

Psalm 139:1-5 - O LORD, you have searched me and known me! You know when I sit down and when I rise up; you discern my thoughts from afar. You search out my path and my lying down and are acquainted with all my ways. Even before a word is on my tongue, behold, O LORD, you know it altogether. You hem me in, behind and before, and lay your hand upon me.

Psalm 63:1 - O God, you are my God; earnestly I seek you; my soul thirsts for you; my flesh faints for you, as in a dry and weary land where there is no water.

Psalm 9:10 - And those who know your name put their trust in you, for you, O LORD, have not forsaken those who seek you.

Willingness produces a desire to seek Him. If we seek Him He will always be found.

1. Seeking – means to search out. Seeking requires time and persistence – set aside a place and time to seek Him. Where and when will that be?

2. Take time today to sit at His feet as you contemplate the above scriptures. Journal any "God Thoughts" of that time.

Day 4

Psalm 46:10-11 - "Be still, and know that I am God. I will be exalted among the nations, I will be exalted in the earth!" The LORD of hosts is with us; the God of Jacob is our fortress. Selah

Isaiah 40:31 - but they who wait for the LORD shall renew their strength; they shall mount up with wings like eagles; they shall run and not be weary; they shall walk and not faint.

Being still requires just that – stillness. No praying, no talking just a place of expectant listening. In a society where input is constant - to be still is often mind-boggling; we no longer know how to be still. If you find yourself in that place take a deep breath and allow a willingness to grow as you step into a new discipline of stillness and listening.

1. How can you make a choice today to become one who lives a lifestyle of stillness, waiting and listening for the voice of your Lord?

2. List some ways to practically apply that choice.

Day 5

Romans 8:28 - And we know that for those who love God all things work together for good, for those who are called according to his purpose.

I Corinthians 2:9 - But, as it is written, "What no eye has seen, nor ear heard, nor the heart of man imagined, what God has prepared for those who love him"

Ephesians 2:22 - In him you also are being built together into a dwelling place for God by the Spirit.

Matthew 13:16 - But blessed are your eyes, for they see, and your ears, for they hear.

To see and hear our Lords voice begins to show forth a yielded life. Trust is required as we begin to say "Yes Lord" to directions and plans as they begin to bubble up within our hearts, minds and spirits.

Stepping forth in boldness to see transformation in our environment only comes from a truly surrendered individual.

1. As this week has progressed and you have begun to be still and listen – what has the Holy Spirit been directing you toward?

2. Are there steps to take and if so what would they be?

3. Implement a step toward that today – if nothing has presented to your heart, mind or spirit yet then take time again today to wait and listen.

Day 6

Isaiah 32:15-18 - until the Spirit is poured upon us from on high, and the wilderness becomes a fruitful field, and the fruitful field is deemed a forest. Then justice will dwell in the wilderness, and righteousness abide in the fruitful field. And the effect of righteousness will be peace, and the result of righteousness, quietness and trust forever. My people will abide in a peaceful habitation, in secure dwellings, and in quiet resting places.

Isaiah 26:3-4 -You keep him in perfect peace whose mind is stayed on you, because he trusts in you. Trust in the LORD forever, for the LORD GOD is an everlasting rock.

The result of stillness and waiting on the Lord always will result in peace.

Re-read *Nature's Surrender – Early Yielders.*

1. What changes have you felt in your spirit this week as you have begun the journey of an Early Yielder – one who trusts, seeks, waits, is still and listens to the Lord?

2. Enjoy quiet time today sitting in the Presence of your King. Listen to His voice and allow a thankful heart to stir delight in His love and promises for you.

You are His Beloved!

The Woodpeckers Single Focus

The early fall morning awakens to the encroaching fog that shrouds the day with stillness and an atmosphere of peace.

Interruption begins as a distinct "tap, tap, tap" beckons for attention.

The previous stillness gives way to this persistent sound.

Hearing the abrupt repetitive wood taping sound reverberating in a consistent cycle of three "tap, tap, tap"s begins to draw me into a search for this lone woodpecker.

The resounding cycle continues, seeming to fill the entire valley with its declaration of presence.

Searching tree to tree I finally see our little driller. This little red headed culprit takes no notice of me for I am not his concern.

This lone woodpecker has a single focus and purpose. To establish and declare his territory as well as attracting appropriate attention for his ultimate design. These purposes are clearly set before him.

This little guy has a single focus and declaration to pursue the call that nature instilled within him and he is a great example of God's plan for you.

As you walk daily under the Lordship and reign of Christ your focus will become singular. The voice of your Lord will begin to resound within you as He directs your purpose. The establishing of His territory in your life, through your life and into others lives will become a declaration of His Kingdom.

Join me as we become like the woodpecker with a single focus yielded and moldable to His purposes.

Day 1

Spend some time contemplating what *The Woodpeckers Single Focus* means to you.

1. What does this mean to you?

2. How does it apply to your life?

Day 2

Proverbs 4:25-26 - Let your eyes look directly forward, and your gaze be straight before you. Ponder the path of your feet; then all your ways will be sure.

Isaiah 32:8 - But he who is noble plans noble things, and on noble things he stands.

Isaiah 55:11 – so shall my word be that goes out from my mouth it shall not return to me empty, but it shall accomplish that which I purpose, and shall succeed in the thing for which I sent it.

When you have entered a place where Jesus is Lord of your life you have yielded to His call. His voice has ultimate say in your life and your purpose is to do His will. Your desire is to make your "daddy" smile.

Just as the woodpecker focused on what he was called to do – you begin a life journey filled with eyes that look forward to the finish line.

1. How would you personally explain being single focused?

2. In what areas of your life do you experience a place of single focus?

3. Are those areas ones that you walk in under the direction of the Holy Spirit? If not – spend time at the feet of Jesus today yielding those areas to His control. Journal your thoughts.

Day 3

Matthew 21:21-22 - And Jesus answered them, "Truly, I say to you, if you have faith and do not doubt, you will not only do what has been done to the fig tree, but even if you say to this mountain, 'Be taken up and thrown into the sea,' it will happen. And whatever you ask in prayer, you will receive, if you have faith."

Hebrews 11:1 - Now faith is the assurance of things hoped for, the conviction of things not seen.

II Corinthians 5:7 – for we walk by faith, not by sight.

A single purpose and focus draws you to a deeper experience of faith. He has called you, He has spoken and He is faithful. That which was once a thought now blooms into an assurance and from that place all things are possible.

A new freedom emerges as this walk of faith begins to express itself. As you hear His voice you respond.

1. Wait at the feet of Jesus today. Listen and respond as He stirs your faith to step out, love touch and pray for people and circumstances that require His hand. Journal your "God Time".

Day 4

Job 42:2 – I know that you can do all things, and that no purpose of yours can be thwarted.

John 14:12-14 - "Truly, truly, I say to you, whoever believes in me will also do the works that I do; and greater works than these will he do, because I am going to the Father. Whatever you ask in my name, this I will do, that the Father may be glorified in the Son. If you ask me anything in my name, I will do it.

John 15:7 - If you abide in me, and my words abide in you, ask whatever you wish, and it will be done for you.

As you walk in a place of yielding to the Lordship of Christ your faith will arise and declarations of it will begin to change your environment.

1. What current situations do you need to see a miracle in?

2. Take them to the feet of Jesus and allow His direction to become apparent within your spirit. Lay them down and trust that He is in charge. Watch as He declares restoration and healing over your life. Journal your thoughts.

Day 5

Jeremiah 29:11 - For I know the plans I have for you, declares the LORD, plans for welfare and not for evil, to give you a future and a hope.

Psalm 138:8 – The Lord will fulfill his purpose for me; your steadfast love, O Lord, endures forever.

Isaiah 54:2 – "Enlarge the place of your tent, and let the curtains of your habitations be stretched out; do not hold back; lengthen your cords and strengthen your stakes.

Just as the woodpecker has a very specific territory and purpose to fulfill in his life so do you. Our Lord has a pre-designed purpose for your life to fulfill. When you become a laid down, willing, moldable, yielded vessel He will rush in and move you into His planned purposes for your life.

You need not worry, struggle or strive to make this happen. Listen and obey is all that is required.

1. As this week has progressed have you begun to hear or see a new direction or a confirmation of a previous purpose? What were they?

2. Spend time listening to His voice today. Journal your "God Time".

<u>Day 6</u>

I Corinthians 7:17 - Only let each person lead the life that the Lord has assigned to him, and to which God has called him. This is my rule in all the churches.

Re-read <u>*The Woodpeckers Single Focus.*</u>

1. What keys have you found this week that can catapult you into a new dimension of faith and purpose?

You are created in His Image!

Yield to the Call and Open the Door

You stand looking in from the outside at this house made of glass. The winds begin to howl and rains splash coldly over your head. You can see the huge glowing rock fireplace with a roaring crackling fire within its hearth. You know it will be warm and dry inside. You know that you have access to its presence. The choice is up to you. It only requires you to open the door.

The choice is made and the door glides open as a whole new adventure materializes before you. What you thought is nothing like it is. There is warmth beyond imagination. The sound of the fire that you had never heard now crackles and sizzles igniting your senses. The smell you could never have experienced before now swirls around your head as smoke and wood meld together in this new atmosphere.

All that you thought you understood about this experience has now exploded into a new inexpressible encounter at the feet of Jesus.

Have you come into this house? Have you chosen to open the door?

Whether you have never known Jesus or have been in or out of the church for years that door can be opened with a simple choice.

Many of you within the church for a lifetime have continued to stand on the outside of this glass house. Looking longingly at the fire, thinking you understand it but never partaking of all that is there and offered to you free of charge.

Don't wait – yield to the call to open that door and walk into a new life free to enjoy all that He has already paid for just for you. Walk into a NEW experience at the feet of Jesus as the Holy Spirit opens your eyes to His presence.

Day 1

Spend some time contemplating what *Yield to the Call and Open the Door* means to you.

1. What does this mean to you?

2. How does it apply to your life?

Day 2

James 1:17 - Every good gift and every perfect gift is from above, coming down from the Father of lights with whom there is no variation or shadow due to change.

Ephesians 1:11-14 - In him we have obtained an inheritance, having been predestined according to the purpose of him who works all things according to the counsel of his will, so that we who were the first to hope in Christ might be to the praise of his glory. In him you also, when you heard the word of truth, the gospel of your salvation, and believed in him, were sealed with the promised Holy Spirit, who is the guarantee of our inheritance until we acquire possession of it, to the praise of his glory.

Matthew 25:1-13 - "Then the kingdom of heaven will be like ten virgins who took their lamps and went to meet the bridegroom. Five of them were foolish, and five were wise. For when the foolish took their lamps, they took no oil with them, but the wise took flasks of oil with their lamps. As the bridegroom was delayed, they all became drowsy and slept. But at midnight there was a cry, 'Here is the bridegroom! Come out to meet him.' Then all those virgins rose and trimmed their lamps.

And the foolish said to the wise, 'Give us some of your oil, for our lamps are going out.' But the wise answered, saying, 'Since there will not be enough for us and for you, go rather to the dealers and buy for yourselves.' And while they were going to buy, the bridegroom came, and those who were ready went in with him to the marriage feast, and the door was shut. Afterward the other virgins came also, saying, 'Lord, lord, open to us.' But he answered, 'Truly, I say to you, I do not know you.' Watch therefore, for you know neither the day nor the hour.

You have been given an inheritance that is far beyond your comprehension. You see it as a house of glass that you stand outside of but the ability to open the door and walk inside and receive its unimaginable benefits lays often just beyond your grasp. His promise for access just has to be accepted. There is so much more to experience in His presence as you yield to His stirrings.

Accept the offer and be ready to walk in that open door.

1. Allow the above scriptures to speak to your heart. Do you understand the great inheritance that you have access to? Are you prepared and ready to enter the door into His presence?

2. What does it mean to you to walk in His inheritance?

3. How can you be prepared and ready to open the door into His presence?

Day 3

Psalm 84:1-2 - How lovely is your dwelling place, O LORD of hosts! My soul longs, yes, faints for the courts of the LORD; my heart and flesh sing for joy to the living God.

Jeremiah 29:13 - You will seek me and find me, when you seek me with all your heart.

Matthew 7:7-8 - "Ask, and it will be given to you; seek, and you will find; knock, and it will be opened to you. For everyone who asks receives, and the one who seeks finds, and to the one who knocks it will be opened.

Psalm 27:4 - One thing have I asked of the LORD, that will I seek after: that I may dwell in the house of the LORD all the days of my life, to gaze upon the beauty of the LORD and to inquire in his temple.

James 4:8 - Draw near to God, and he will draw near to you. Cleanse your hands, you sinners, and purify your hearts, you double-minded.

Hebrews 4:16 - Let us then with confidence draw near to the throne of grace, that we may receive mercy and find grace to help in time of need.

Access into the presence of God begins with the Holy Spirit (who dwells within each believer) who stirs a love and desire for a deeper "face to face" encounter with our Lord. As you spend more time at the feet of Jesus that desire will grow and will draw you into a place where MORE of Him and LESS of you will prepare you for new things.

1. Spend time today contemplating the above scriptures. How would you describe your current level of "asking, seeking and drawing near" to God?

Day 4

John 10:9-10 - I am the door. If anyone enters by me, he will be saved and will go in and out and find pasture. The thief comes only to steal and kill and destroy. I came that they may have life and have it abundantly.

Ephesians 2:18 - For through him we both have access in one Spirit to the Father.

Hebrews 6:19 - We have this as a sure and steadfast anchor of the soul, a hope that enters into the inner place behind the curtain,

Revelation 3:20 - Behold, I stand at the door and knock. If anyone hears my voice and opens the door, I will come in to him and eat with him, and he with me.

You carry an open door within your very spirit that connects you as a "born again believer in Jesus" to a deep place of knowing your Lord. It is a promise that you already have received. No begging, groveling or earning is required.

The yielded heart that proclaims "YES LORD" sees and experiences that open door into His unsearchable inheritance.

It is already yours, so walk through the door with confidence.

1. Take time today to sit at the feet of Jesus, soak in His presence, listen to His voice and rejoice in your inheritance. Journal your "God Time".

Day 5

Hebrews 12:28-29 - Therefore let us be grateful for receiving a kingdom that cannot be shaken, and thus let us offer to God acceptable worship, with reverence and awe, for our God is a consuming fire.

Psalm 16:11 - You make known to me the path of life; in your presence there is fullness of joy; at your right hand are pleasures forevermore.

Revelation 7:17 - For the Lamb in the midst of the throne will be their shepherd, and he will guide them to springs of living water, and God will wipe away every tear from their eyes."

1 Corinthians 2:9-12 - But, as it is written, "What no eye has seen, nor ear heard, nor the heart of man imagined, what God has prepared for those who love him"— these things God has revealed to us through the Spirit. For the Spirit searches everything, even the depths of God. For who knows a person's thoughts except the spirit of that person, which is in him? So also no one comprehends the thoughts of God except the Spirit of God. Now we have received not the spirit of the world, but the Spirit who is from God, that we might understand the things freely given us by God.

Romans 11:33 - Oh, the depth of the riches and wisdom and knowledge of God! How unsearchable are his judgments and how inscrutable his ways!

The depths of your Lord and all that He has to pour out on you can never be fully experienced in a lifetime. You have a promise of an inheritance that you can - as a yielded vessel - walk momentarily in on this earth but it is only a glimpse of what is to come. It is a gift that you have access to right now. It is your choice to yield to His call and open that door.

1. Take time today to write out at least 5 things that you have been shown as to the great, unsearchable mysteries of Christ – either through the word or personal experience.

2. Spend time rejoicing in HOW GREAT IS OUR LORD.

Day 6

Re-read *Yield to the Call and Open the Door.*

1. Summarize the revelations you received this week as you spent time in the word and at His feet.

You are His Chosen Heir!

Let Him Sweep Up the Mess

Let's watch as a neighbor begins a remodeling process of his yard and drive way.

First comes the "un-doing".

The jackhammers begin to vibrate the area as breaking through the previously poured concrete begins. The air continues to resound with the process - as the pounding of hammers joins in the crescendo. Next comes the bringing down of the block walled fencing with thuds and shacking of the earth. Trucks arrive with backhoes and added helpers as the tearing and ripping out of the old shrubs and grass joins the process.

Days of noise continue to fill the previously quiet street. The once familiar view is now in chaos as activity reigns.

Suddenly, one morning we awake to silence once again. Upon looking - the dust has settled but what is viewed now is a yard full of rubble. The day continues in silence and when day two gives silently away to the sound of crickets we began to wonder. "Is it possible they have no plans for re-building?"

As the sun begins to warm the dust on the third morning we find one silent worker – the neighbor – with a broom and a wheelbarrow. He works diligently all day clearing all the brokenness that has been accomplished during the de-construction phase.

Let's ponder this process. We too require an "un-doing" phase in our lives as well as a clean up and re-building.

During our spiritual life journey we encounter hurts and offences, which cause us to build walls of protection that surround our hearts. Those offences and hurts can be legitimate and some trivial but the walls become thicker and thicker as time moves on.

In order to be free and totally yielded to the call of Christ in our lives we must be willing to set all of these offences and hurts down. This requires an "un-doing" of walls and cracked foundations.

What takes days in the natural only takes a yielded heart in the spiritual. Acknowledging these hurts and offences and being willing to allow the tearing down process to begin will transform your life. You will begin to be free to open up to others, let them in and see a future that was previously hidden behind those walls.

Don't allow fear of "the clean-up" to stop you and keep you hidden behind those walls. It is only your job to say "Yes Lord". He has the broom and wheelbarrow and lovingly will sweep up the mess.

Day 1

Spend some time contemplating what *Let Him Sweep Up the Mess* means to you.

1. What does this mean to you?

2. How does it apply to your life?

Day 2

Proverbs 10:11-12 - The mouth of the righteous is a fountain of life, but the mouth of the wicked conceals violence. Hatred stirs up strife, but love covers all offenses.

Psalm 133:1 - Behold, how good and pleasant it is when brothers dwell in unity!

Luke 8:17 - For nothing is hidden that will not be made manifest, nor is anything secret that will not be known and come to light.

Stepping into a new place of freedom in Christ requires acknowledgement and willingness to drop your walls of offense and protection. You are not alone, for we all have been on both sides of offence and are good at constructing protection around a hurt heart. Yielding those to the Lordship of Jesus Christ and allowing that pain to be transformed by the renewing of your mind through the Holy Spirit is the beginning of a newfound freedom.

1. What areas of offence and walls of protection have you built?

2. Take time to write them down on a separate piece of paper. Now take that paper and make a choice to shred it up.

3. Acknowledge those shredded papers at the feet of Jesus today and begin the healing process. Journal your thoughts.

Day 3

Hosea 10:12 - Sow for yourselves righteousness; reap steadfast love; break up your fallow ground, for it is the time to seek the LORD, that he may come and rain righteousness upon you.

Luke 14:28 - For which of you, desiring to build a tower, does not first sit down and count the cost, whether he has enough to complete it?

Matthew 19:26 - But Jesus looked at them and said, "With man this is impossible, but with God all things are possible."

Acknowledging the walls will allow you the opportunity to step into a place where you can totally yield those situations at the cross. Then what is impossible for you to do for yourself begins to occur. The Holy Spirit comes in and tears down long standing walls. He comes in and pours righteousness upon you and restores what was stolen thus bringing life, joy and freedom.

1. Spend time today at the feet of your Lord – give Him full access as you pour out the hurts and offences. Then in a waiting – **silent -** posture before Him – focus on the promise of restoration. Journal your thoughts.

Day 4

Isaiah 41:13 - For I, the LORD your God, hold your right hand; it is I who say to you, "Fear not, I am the one who helps you."

II Timothy 1:7 - for God gave us a spirit not of fear but of power and love and self-control.

1 John 4:18 - There is no fear in love, but perfect love casts out fear. For fear has to do with punishment, and whoever fears has not been perfected in love.

Psalm 34:4 - I sought the LORD, and he answered me and delivered me from all my fears.

Often when you are presented with painful memories and offences the first thoughts are "nope-not going there" Or "I am such a mess – if I open this can of worms I will never be whole again" and many such thoughts. You again, are not alone in these fears. However, yielding to the Lordship of Christ is a process of allowing Him to "open your can of worms" and trusting Him to heal, deliver and restore. Lay down your fear and receive His overwhelming love.

1. What areas are you holding back and not allowing this restoration process full access to?

2. What fears prohibit your willingness?

3. Spend time today at the feet of Jesus presenting the above thoughts to him – journal your thoughts.

Day 5

Psalm 55:22 - Cast your burden on the LORD, and he will sustain you; he will never permit the righteous to be moved.

Psalm 37:23-24 - The steps of a man are established by the LORD, when he delights in his way; though he fall, he shall not be cast headlong, for the LORD upholds his hand.

Proverbs 4:23 - Keep your heart with all vigilance, for from it flow the springs of life.

Galatians 5:1 - For freedom Christ has set us free; stand firm therefore, and do not submit again to a yoke of slavery.

Romans 8:1 - There is therefore now no condemnation for those who are in Christ Jesus.

Proverbs 3:5-6 - Trust in the LORD with all your heart, and do not lean on your own understanding. In all your ways acknowledge him, and he will make straight your paths.

Trusting in the Lord is the key to a true yielding posture. Knowing that He loves you and desires the best for you will allow you to accept His loving restoration process.

Your job is only to say "YES Lord" and He has the broom and wheelbarrow. He will lovingly sweep up the mess.

1. How would you explain your understanding of trust in the Lord?

2. Write down several areas that you know you struggle in trusting Him.

3. Take those to the feet of Jesus today and journal your thoughts.

Day 6

Re-read *Let Him Sweep Up the Mess.*

1. How have you experienced healing, deliverance and restoration this week as you learned to yield to His "undoing' in your life?

You are Victorious in Christ!

Believe in His Faithfulness

Once the clean up of our neighbors yard is complete workers again converge. This time the focus is on the foundation of the driveway. Frames are placed and cement begins to flow. Time and patience is required as the process continues. Curing is temperamental and it will be many days before it can be tested with any weight. Again our street sits silent for days waiting to see how this project will emerge. No activity. No movement. Just anticipation.

Finally, one morning as our blinds are raised we stand stunned by our new view. What yesterday was barren is new today. The sun glistens off of dewy blades of grass and beautifully manicured shrubs and trees in our neighbors yard.

"How can that be?" we question. "These things don't just happen, they take hard work".

We see but don't believe. In fairy-tales and magic shows we see things appear and disappear. When the stunning assistant is covered with a black bag and placed into a locked chest she now instantly disappears. What was a pumpkin and mice becomes a carriage and beautiful stallions. We see but don't believe. We believe in masters of illusion and special affects.

Looking at our spiritual walk we expect that hard work is required from us to achieve any change. We must do it.

However, once our choice to say "Yes Lord" takes place Christ steps in and cleans up the mess of our lives.

A new foundation begins. This foundation does take some time, some patience and trusting in the process. But all the glory comes as He unveils what was hidden inside of you. The fresh laid grass and beautifully manicured shrubs appear. The pumpkin and mice DO instantly become something new. The box that was once filled of our sins, hurts and offences IS empty.

Our willingness to yield to His Lordship brings His reign – His yield of abundance and change into our lives.

Allow this process in your life to materialize as you daily walk under His reign and watch as old things become new – Believe in His faithfulness.

Day 1

Spend some time contemplating what *Believe in His Faithfulness* means to you.

1. What does this mean to you?

2. How does it apply to your life?

Day 2

Hebrews 3:4 - (For every house is built by someone, but the builder of all things is God.)

Hebrews 11:10 - For he was looking forward to the city that has foundations, whose designer and builder is God.

Proverbs 24:3 - By wisdom a house is built, and by understanding it is established;

Isaiah 28:16 - therefore thus says the Lord GOD, "Behold, I am the one who has laid as a foundation in Zion, a stone, a tested stone, a precious cornerstone, of a sure foundation: 'Whoever believes will not be in haste.'

Knowing that your foundation and builder is Jesus and that His plans for your life are plans that are filled with a purpose makes the yielding process one filled with faith and trust in His love for you. Spending time both in His presence as well as His word strengthen that "knowing" within.

Allowing the presence of Christ to have full reign and Lordship as old foundations are demolished requires patience and trust. He is faithful to restore and rebuild as you wait at His feet.

1. What do the above scriptures of promise mean to you as you learn to trust Him to rebuild a sure foundation in your life?

2. Spend time today both in His presence and in reading the bible.

3. Journal your thoughts from your time with Him today.

Day 3

Psalm 127:1- Unless the LORD builds the house, those who build it labor in vain. Unless the LORD watches over the city, the watchman stays awake in vain.

Ephesians 2:8-9 - For by grace you have been saved through faith. And this is not your own doing; it is the gift of God, not a result of works, so that no one may boast.

Patiently waiting for things to happen is not a strong suit for humans. Trying to speed the process by intervening is laboring in vain. It is not your place to figure out or help hurry the foundation and work that Jesus is doing in your life. Resting in the process is also part of stepping into a life that walks in freedom under the reign of Christ's Lordship.

1. Where do you find yourself often frustrated in this resting process?

2. Take time today to listen for new encouragement from the Holy Spirit as you sit at the feet of Jesus. Journal your "God Thoughts".

Day 4

II Corinthians 3:18 – And we all, with unveiled face, beholding the glory of the Lord, are being transformed into the same image from one degree of glory to another. For this comes from the Lord who is the Spirit.

1 Peter 2:4-5 - As you come to him, a living stone rejected by men but in the sight of God chosen and precious, you yourselves like living stones are being built up as a spiritual house, to be a holy priesthood, to offer spiritual sacrifices acceptable to God through Jesus Christ.

Hebrews 10:23 – Let us hold fast the confession of our hope without wavering, for he who promised is faithful.

Psalms 36:5-9 - Your steadfast love, O Lord, extends to the heavens, your faithfulness to the clouds. Your righteousness is like the mountains of God; your judgments are like the great deep; man and beast you save, O Lord. How precious is your steadfast love, O God! The children of mankind take refuge in the shadow of your wings. They feast on the abundance of your house, and you give them drink from the river of your delights. For with you is the fountain of life; in your light do we see light.

Ezekiel 36:26 - And I will give you a new heart, and a new spirit I will put within you. And I will remove the heart of stone from your flesh and give you a heart of flesh.

He who is faithful has promised you a life that in an instant can be transformed. BELIEVE in His promises and step into a life of abundant freedom.

As you walk a yielded life your purpose as a child of God will shine through as you pour out His glory. You will become a vessel that is continually transformed from one glory to another as you walk this new journey.

1. What is your understanding of being transformed from glory to glory?

2. Describe what that would look like in your personal life.

Day 5

Joel 2:25-26 - I will restore to you the years that the swarming locust has eaten, the hopper, the destroyer, and the cutter, my great army, which I sent among you. "You shall eat in plenty and be satisfied, and praise the name of the LORD your God, who has dealt wondrously with you. And my people shall never again be put to shame.

Acts 20:32 - And now I commend you to God and to the word of his grace, which is able to build you up and to give you the inheritance among all those who are sanctified.

Often when we begin this yielding lifestyle it requires much to be laid at the feet of Jesus.

During this process you may have seen destruction that has been un-earthed as the process has unfolded. Stand strong for your Lord is your Redeemer. Believe in His promises and you will see your life filled with abundance.

1. Take time today at the feet of Jesus with a thankful heart regarding the above promises of restoration?

2. Journal your thoughts of things you are thankful for?

Day 6

Re-read *Believe in His Faithfulness.*

1. As you have waited at the feet of Jesus this week what revelations have been revealed?

2. Summarize your understanding of this weeks study?

You are Righteous in Christ!

Abundant Fruit Happens in a Yielded Life

Fall brings with it a natural yielding process full of abundant goodness as we look forward to the harvesting of its provision.

With love and care the gardener has watered, fertilized, pruned and prepared throughout the warm summer months. His focus and attention has been in anticipation for what will be produced upon his vines and trees as fall approaches.

As his vines and fruit trees grow heavy with abundant fruit, preparation to consume and preserve their bounty kicks into high gear all around him. The sheer joy of the overflowing fragrant ripeness of these fruits permeates and stirs us to action. We climb, gather, wash, sort and share as we look forward to pies to be made, jams to be canned and juices to be squeezed.

We enjoy the bounty that is poured forth from the hand of the gardener who has done all the cultivating for our benefit. What an abundant blessing of His yield has been given to us!

Spiritually, we have a master gardener who has done the watering, fertilizing, pruning and preparing. Watching and waiting for the fruit to burst forth in our lives.

As we yield to His Lordship and live under His reign – fruit happens.

We yield to Him and He pours an abundant yield into and through our lives.

Join me as we enjoy and share those fruits – being ready to pour them out to everyone we encounter.

Day 1

Spend some time contemplating what *Abundant Fruit Happens in a Yielded Life* means to you.

1. What does this mean to you?

2. How does it apply to your life?

Day 2

1 Peter 5:6-7 - Humble yourselves, therefore, under the mighty hand of God so that at the proper time he may exalt you, casting all your anxieties on him, because he cares for you.

Psalm 23:6 – Surely goodness and mercy shall follow me all the days of my life, and I shall dwell in the house of the Lord forever.

Luke 8:15 - As for that in the good soil, they are those who, hearing the word, hold it fast in an honest and good heart, and bear fruit with patience.

As you humble yourself – yield – under the Lordship of Jesus all of life changes. All the weeds – old thinking and attitudes – begin to disappear. Jesus – the master gardener prepares you for a harvest of abundance.

1. Where do you find yourself now – have you come to a place where your life has been yielded to His Lordship?

2. Over the last several months what preparations have been done in your life? (Weeding, watering, fertilizing and pruning) How would you relate those to the gardening preparations we provide in our natural gardens? Journal your thoughts.

Day 3

II Peter 1:3 - His divine power has granted to us all things that pertain to life and godliness, through the knowledge of him who called us to his own glory and excellence,

Psalm 1:3 - He is like a tree planted by streams of water that yields its fruit in its season, and its leaf does not wither. In all that he does, he prospers.

As you lay down under the Lordship of Christ you become the person you were designed to be. You flourish and grow in areas you never imagined as doors begin to open before you. His time, His provisions, His joy and all that is GOOD begins to flow over and through you.

Do I mean life is always "sunny"? Nope, not at all; however, when your focus is consistently directed at His feet you walk in peace. His face, His plans, His directions and the deep-seated faith within you will move you differently. With a yielded heart and eyes filled with love for your Lord you will find yourself focused forward to His plans not yours and abundant fruit will emerge.

1. Take time today to rejoice in the abundance of His life that is poured into yours. List at least 10 things that you are thankful for.

2. Sit at His feet today and bask in His goodness. Journal your "God Time".

Day 4

Isaiah 4:2 - In that day the branch of the LORD shall be beautiful and glorious, and the fruit of the land shall be the pride and honor of the survivors of Israel.

Galatians 5:22-23 - But the fruit of the Spirit is love, joy, peace, patience, kindness, goodness, faithfulness, gentleness, self-control; against such things there is no law.

Matthew 7:16 - You will recognize them by their fruits. Are grapes gathered from thorn bushes, or figs from thistles?

As you continue this amazing journey under the reign of Christ you will begin to produce fruit that will be obvious.

1. Contemplate Galatians 5:22-23 above. Do you see some of these fruits beginning to grow in your life? Which ones?

2. Take time today to sit "silently" with Jesus - Journal this time.

Day 5

II Corinthians 9:8 - And God is able to make all grace abound to you, so that having all sufficiency in all things at all times, you may abound in every good work.

II Corinthians 10:13 - But we will not boast beyond limits, but will boast only with regard to the area of influence God assigned to us, to reach even to you.

II Corinthians 2:14-17 - But thanks be to God, who in Christ always leads us in triumphal procession, and through us spreads the fragrance of the knowledge of him everywhere. For we are the aroma of Christ to God among those who are being saved and among those who are perishing, to one a fragrance from death to death, to the other a fragrance from life to life. Who is sufficient for these things? For we are not, like so many, peddlers of God's word, but as men of sincerity, as commissioned by God, in the sight of God we speak in Christ.

Galatians 2:20 - I have been crucified with Christ. It is no longer I who live, but Christ who lives in me. And the life I now live in the flesh I live by faith in the Son of God, who loved me and gave himself for me.

What a joy it is to be given an assignment from your Lord! As you walk in a yielded lifestyle where you are consistently tuned into the voice of the Spirit of God you will be directed to step out and into His purposes. His plan is always for you to pour out the love of Christ on a broken lost world. Jesus is the only answer we have for those around you.

You are commissioned by God to speak of Christ and His free gift of forgiveness and love.

Step out – pour out in love to those you encounter. They are lost, broken and lonely and you have the assignment to share your fruit.

1. Who are those around you that don't know the love of Christ?

2. Begin to take that list to the feet of Jesus and ask for open doors and opportunities to speak for Him. Journal your thoughts, directions and answers to these prayers as you watch Him use your fruit?

Day 6

Re-read *Abundant Fruit Happens in a Yielded Life.*

1. What revelations from scriptures, the prose writing, your personal time with God and your journaling have you received this week?

2. Summarize the impact these will make on your life.

You are Highly Favored!

The Faithful Evergreen's Canopy

As fall commences the barren trees and vines lapse into sleep as the season approaches. However, the evergreen fir continues to declare her-self. Nature's now bleak landscape is vibrant and alive because of her presence just as every season before. She provides a canopy in every region from the ocean to the desert.

Year after year the evergreen stands as a sentry on a wall. Her innate knowledge of natures design buried deep within. She pours out to us a gift that is often enjoyed and received with no acknowledgment.

The evergreen yields as season after season passes.

Winter covers her with frost and snow, as well as biting winds that bend and rip at her branches. Spring brings new life as many birds enjoy her outstretched support and protection as nests of babies flourish. Summer rushes in with beating unrelenting sun and heat. But the evergreen stands strong bringing shade to humans and animals alike. Fall begins and gives relief to her as rains begin to pour forth and she yields to their refreshing.

Even through disasters – fires, landslides and more - those you see still standing often are the branchless, charred and bent – stately, faithful, yielding evergreens.

Similarly, we desire to walk through our spiritual life journey declaring the same.

Our faith in Christ and His design for our lives is our primary focus. As we trust in the invisible – we begin to know that He is always for us. His love draws us to a place where our desire to be who we are created to be gives rise within us to pour out that love back to our "daddy". Knowing who we are in Him grows that desire not to present anything back to Him out of obligation but because we love Him so much we want to make Him smile. We no longer need to be noticed by others but do what He directs and that is what drives our lives.

We begin to allow our branches to carry the frost, snow and winds both for ourselves and for others. We lift up life and speak encouragement always. We stand in faith as the heat scorches. We bring shade to those we encounter and love. As fall approaches we yield again to His call and His direction. Year after year growing stronger and deeper in faith. We are always ready for the next season.

The yielding process is not one that occurs once and is done. It is a life journey that begins and continues to grow as we willingly set aside our ways and accept His. Listening to His voice and season after season we stand on that voice.

Join me in this amazing journey - where it is always MORE of Him and LESS of me.

Day 1

Spend some time contemplating what *The Faithful Evergreen's Canopy* means to you.

1. What does this mean to you?

2. How does it apply to your life?

Day 2

Romans 1:16-17 - For I am not ashamed of the gospel, for it is the power of God for salvation to everyone who believes, to the Jew first and also to the Greek. For in it the righteousness of God is revealed from faith for faith, as it is written, "The righteous shall live by faith."

Philippians 3:8-9 - Indeed, I count everything as loss because of the surpassing worth of knowing Christ Jesus my Lord. For his sake I have suffered the loss of all things and count them as rubbish, in order that I may gain Christ and be found in him, not having a righteousness of my own that comes from the law, but that which comes through faith in Christ, the righteousness from God that depends on faith—

Your faith and trust in who Jesus Christ is and who He has created you to be is the root on which your journey will stand as season upon season passes.

The faith that lives deep within your core is one you stand upon - a faith from which you can't be shaken. This faith arises from knowing and trusting in an invisible God.

1. Write out a simple personal statement of your own understanding and meaning of faith in Christ.

2. Do others around you know that you are a follower of Christ? Do you speak freely and openly of your faith?

3. Spend time today at the feet of Jesus and contemplate your answers above. Journal your thoughts.

Day 3

Isaiah 58:11 - And the LORD will guide you continually and satisfy your desire in scorched places and make your bones strong; and you shall be like a watered garden, like a spring of water, whose waters do not fail.

1 John 3:16 - By this we know love, that he laid down his life for us, and we ought to lay down our lives for the brothers.

Philippians 4:8 -Finally, brothers, whatever is true, whatever is honorable, whatever is just, whatever is pure, whatever is lovely, whatever is commendable, if there is any excellence, if there is anything worthy of praise, think about these things.

Walking daily in a yielded listening posture before your Lord requires a deep awareness of where your strength comes from and a willingness to lay down your plans on behalf of someone else.

The yielding process is never done and you will find yourself daily laying down thoughts, attitudes and selfishness. However having a willing spirit and a desire to please "daddy" is what brings a smile to His face and freedom to yours.

1. Where and how do you receive strength?

2. Think of a time over the past few weeks where you listened to His direction and laid aside your plans and reached out to another. How did you feel?

3. Clearing our minds is an easy "refresh" – Using Philippians 4:8 (above) write out several things that you can think on that are (honorable, just, pure, lovely, commendable, excellent, and praise worthy).

4. Enjoy some time at the feet of Jesus and journal your thoughts.

Day 4

1 Peter 3:15 - but in your hearts honor Christ the Lord as holy, always being prepared to make a defense to anyone who asks you for a reason for the hope that is in you; yet do it with gentleness and respect,

1 Corinthians 15:58 - Therefore, my beloved brothers, be steadfast, immovable, always abounding in the work of the Lord, knowing that in the Lord your labor is not in vain.

Romans 15:1-7 - We who are strong have an obligation to bear with the failings of the weak, and not to please ourselves. Let each of us please his neighbor for his good, to build him up. For Christ did not please himself, but as it is written, "The reproaches of those who reproached you fell on me." For whatever was written in former days was written for our instruction, that through endurance and through the encouragement of the Scriptures we might have hope. May the God of endurance and encouragement grant you to live in such harmony with one another, in accord with Christ Jesus, that together you may with one voice glorify the God and Father of our Lord Jesus Christ. Therefore welcome one another as Christ has welcomed you, for the glory of God.

Having a willing ear to hear your Lord will often place you in the right place at the right time. You become an answer to prayers both unspoken and spoken. Ready with a simple smile, words of encouragement and love you are the living example of Jesus love for those you come in contact with.

Walking in this lifestyle is never boring. Begin to ask Him to use you every day. He will pour His love through you into others. He is always faithful. The lost and lonely are everywhere – the grocery store, the gas station, the line at the pizza place – etc. etc. Where you go He goes. Willingness to watch, listen and speak becomes an adventure.

1. Practice the above admonishment. Journal your experience.

Day 5

Isaiah 61: 1-6 - The Spirit of the Lord God is upon me, because the Lord has anointed me to bring good news to the poor; he has sent me to bind up the brokenhearted, to proclaim liberty to the captives,
and the opening of the prison to those who are bound; to proclaim the year of the Lord's favor, and the day of vengeance of our God; to comfort all who mourn; to grant to those who mourn in Zion—
to give them a beautiful headdress instead of ashes, the oil of gladness instead of mourning, the garment of praise instead of a faint spirit; that they may be called oaks of righteousness, the planting of the Lord, that he may be glorified. They shall build up the ancient ruins; they shall raise up the former devastations; they shall repair the ruined cities, the devastations of many generations. Strangers shall stand and tend your flocks; foreigners shall be your plowmen and vinedressers; but you shall be called the priests of the Lord; they shall speak of you as the ministers of our God; you shall eat the wealth of the nations, and in their glory you shall boast.

Galatians 6:9-10 - And let us not grow weary of doing good, for in due season we will reap, if we do not give up. So then, as we have opportunity, let us do good to everyone, and especially to those who are of the household of faith.

I Thessalonians 5:11 – Therefore encourage one another and build one another up, just as you are doing.

Your yielded life brings the glory of the Lord to those around you. Carrying burdens, proclaiming liberty, binding up broken hearts, encouraging are all works of Jesus. As His yielded vessels you too are doing those works in His name. Through a life that pours out love – no judgment, no opinions – just love - you will bring light to the darkest areas and see freedom reign in many lives.

1. Spend time at the feet of Jesus today and journal any specific directions or thoughts He may stir as you contemplate the above.

Day 6

Ephesians 6:10—20-Finally, be strong in the Lord and in the strength of his might. Put on the whole armor of God, that you may be able to stand against the schemes of the devil. For we do not wrestle against flesh and blood, but against the rulers, against the authorities, against the cosmic powers over this present darkness, against the spiritual forces of evil in the heavenly places. Therefore take up the whole armor of God, that you may be able to withstand in the evil day, and having done all, to stand firm. Stand therefore, having fastened on the belt of truth, and having put on the breastplate of righteousness, and, as shoes for your feet, having put on the readiness given by the gospel of peace. In all circumstances take up the shield of faith, with which you can extinguish all the flaming darts of the evil one; and take the helmet of salvation, and the sword of the Spirit, which is the word of God, praying at all times in the Spirit, with all prayer and supplication. To that end keep alert with all perseverance, making supplication for all the saints, and also for me, that words may be given to me in opening my mouth boldly to proclaim the mystery of the gospel, for which I am an ambassador in chains, that I may declare it boldly, as I ought to speak.

John 3:30 – He must increase, but I must decrease

Philippians 2:1-4 - So if there is any encouragement in Christ, any comfort from love, any participation in the Spirit, any affection and sympathy, complete my joy by being of the same mind, having the same love, being in full accord and of one mind. Do nothing from selfish ambition or conceit, but in humility count others more significant than yourselves. Let each of you look not only to his own interests, but also to the interests of others.

Living a life under the Lordship of Christ brings freedom unimaginable. This journey is one where it must always be MORE of Him and LESS of you.

Re-read *The Faithful Evergreen's Canopy.*

1. Summarize your thoughts about this weeks prose.

2. During the last 3 months how is your life being re-directed to a place of MORE of Him and LESS of you as you live out a yielded life under the Lordship of Jesus?

You are His Beloved!

Notes

Notes

Titles available by J.K. Sanchez

Majestic Reflection Devotional Study Series:

Winters Rest

Spring's Assurance

Summer's Delight

Fall's Yield

Stand alone or companion journals:

Winters Rest Journal

Spring's Assurance Journal

Summer's Delight Journal

Fall's Yield Journal

Majestic Reflection Journal

Reflections of His Glory Journal

Additonal Titles

Reflections of His Glory

Contact me at: Judy@jksanchez.com

Jksanchez.com

About the Author

J. K. Sanchez has lived and raised her three children in the Pacific Northwest where she and her husband of 40 years live and enjoy its beauty. As a writer and photographer her love of nature has flourished and is portrayed both through visually descriptive prose as well as through the eye of the camera.

Having ministered in many areas of the body of Christ her love for people and passion for worship and the presence of the Lord continually draw her to see freedom proclaimed and released to others through the finished work on the cross of Jesus.

www.ingramcontent.com/pod-product-compliance
Lightning Source LLC
Chambersburg PA
CBHW060248050426
42448CB00009B/1594

* 9 7 8 0 6 9 2 4 9 9 4 7 4 *